Even These Things

Rory Mullarkey

methuen | drama

LONDON · NEW YORK · OXFORD · NEW DELHI · SYDNEY

METHUEN DRAMA

Bloomsbury Publishing Plc, 50 Bedford Square, London, WC1B 3DP, UK
Bloomsbury Publishing Inc, 1359 Broadway, New York, NY 10018, USA
Bloomsbury Publishing Ireland, 29 Earlsfort Terrace, Dublin 2,
D02 AY28, Ireland

BLOOMSBURY, METHUEN DRAMA and the Methuen
Drama logo are trademarks of Bloomsbury Publishing Plc.

First published in Great Britain 2026
Reprinted 2026

A catalogue record for this book is available from the British Library.

A catalog record for this book is available from the Library of Congress.

ISBN: PB: 978-1-3506-5992-6
ePDF: 978-1-3506-5993-3
eBook: 978-1-3506-5994-0

Series: Modern Plays

Typeset by Mark Heslington Ltd, Scarborough, North Yorkshire
Printed and bound in Great Britain

For product safety related questions contact
productsafety@bloomsbury.com.

To find out more about our authors and books visit
www.bloomsbury.com and sign up for our newsletters.

Even These Things

Rory Mullarkey

Commissioned and produced by
the Royal Exchange Theatre

First performance of *Even These Things* was at the Royal
Exchange Theatre, Manchester, on 15 May 2026

Even These Things
by Rory Mullarkey

Annie Donovan/Kaz	**Elaine Cassidy**
Jenny	**Katherine Pearce**
Helicopter Pilot/Queen Victoria	**Fionnuala Dorrity**
Little Girl in Angel Costume	**Erynne Harris**
	Mila Rook
	Evelyn Teixeira

WRITER	**Rory Mullarkey**
DIRECTOR	**James Macdonald**
DESIGNER	**Laura Hopkins**
LIGHTING DESIGNER	**Charles Balfour**
SOUND DESIGNER	**Ian Dickinson**
MOVEMENT AND INTIMACY DIRECTOR	**Georgina Lamb**
ACCENT & DIALECT COACH	**Helen Simmons**
CASTING DIRECTOR	**Amy Ball CDG**
CHILDRENS' CASTING DIRECTOR	**Keston & Keston**
DRAMATURG	**Emily McLaughlin**
ASSOCIATE DIRECTOR	**Katie Greenall**
BIRKBECK ASSISTANT DIRECTOR	**Sadie Mears**
ARRANGER AND CHORAL LEADER	**Michael Betteridge**
PRODUCTION MANAGER	**Jacqui Leigh**
STAGE MANAGER	**Sarah Castleton Smith**
DEPUTY STAGE MANAGER	**Alex Burke**
ASSISTANT STAGE MANAGER	**Amelia Blackburn**
ASSISTANT STAGE MANAGER	**T Harris**

With special thanks to:
Splinter Scenery
Theatre Clywd
RPS
Royal & Derngate, Northampton
Octagon Theatre, Bolton
Media Co
Bare Arms

Cast

Elaine Cassidy – Annie Donovan/Kaz

Elaine Cassidy is an award-winning Irish actress who first gained prominence with her leading role in *Disco Pigs* (2001), for which she won the Irish Film and Television Award. Theatre credits include: *Aristocrats, Fathers and Sons* (Donmar Warehouse); *Les Liaisons Dangereuses* (Donmar Warehouse); *Scenes From The Big Picture* (National Theatre); *A Gypsy Riding* (Almeida Theatre); *The Lieutenant of Inishmore, The Crucible* (Royal Shakespeare Company). Television and film credits include: *Felicia's Journey, The Paradise, No Offence, A Room with a View* (BBC); *Sanctuary: A Witch's Tale, The Wonder, The Last Kingdom: Seven Kings Must Die* (Netflix); *The Reformation Of Sister Edith* (Humble Priory); *Belgravia: The Next Chapter* (MGM+).

Katherine Pearce – Jenny

Katherine trained at the Royal Welsh College of Music and Drama. Katherine won a Stage Edinburgh Award for Best Performance for *Island Town* (and was nominated for an Off West End Theatre Award for Low Level Panic). Theatre credits include: *The Merry Wives of Windsor* (Shakespeare's Globe), *Midsummer Night's Dream, King John, The Whip* (Royal Shakespeare Company); *Port, Husbands and Sons* (National Theatre); *Our Pals, No Pay? No Way!* (Royal Exchange Theatre); *Woyzeck, A Streetcar Named Desire, Glitterland, Chamber Piece, A Stab in the Dark, A Series of Increasingly Impossible Acts* (Lyric Hammersmith). Film credits include: *England Is Mine* (HanWay Films) and *My Cousin Rachel* (Fox Searchlight). TV credits include: *Rules of the Game, Three Girls* (BBC); *Girlfriends* (ITV).

Fionnuala Dorrity – Helicopter Pilot/Queen Victoria

Credits include: *The Sailmaker's Palm, Transfigured, Bellmouth Papercone* (Oceanallover); *Not Better, First* (Amadan Ensemble); *Der Schmetterlingseffeckt* (Derevo); *What We Talk About When We Talk About Love* (Erratica Theatre/Soundworlds Podcast); *The Shadow of Heaven* (Al Seed Productions); *The Jungle Book* (Unity Theatre); *In a Pickle* (Oily Cart/Royal Shakespeare Company); *Ring* (Shunt); *Lysistrata* (Watford Palace Theatre); *The Ugly Duckling* (Sheffield Theatres); *Ten Tiny Toes* (Liverpool Everyman); *Out of the Blue* (Rejects' Revenge); *Doctor Faustus* (Third Party); *The Tower of Light, The Lovely Farmers, Noah's Ark* (Walk the Plank); *Soulskin* (Red

Ladder); *You Are The Sun* (Hurly Burly Theatre); *Beautiful Bones* (Surge); *The Corrupted Angel* (Base Chorus/Royal Opera House); *Miss Nobody, Manfred, The Beautiful Ugly, Writing the Century, Yerma* (BBC Radio Drama); *You Kissed Me, Astraeus, Dead Belgian* (self-produced).

Erynne Harris – Little Girl in an Angel Costume

Training: Erynne trains at The Drama MOB in Manchester and is represented by The Drama MOB Management. Erynne has recently filmed a TV commercial for EE.

Mila Rook – Little Girl in an Angel Costume

Training: Mila trains at The Drama MOB drama classes and is represented by The Drama MOB Management. Credits: Samsung TVC, feature film.

Evelyn Teixeira – Little Girl in an Angel Costume

Training: Stagebox, Breakdance Manchester. Credits: *The Next Big Thing is You* (Samsung global brand film), *Fear* (Amazon Prime), *One Day* (Netflix), *Black Doves* (Netflix), *Flavia de Luce* (Sky) and *Paw Petrol* (Nickelodeon).

Creatives

Rory Mullarkey – Writer

Rory grew up in Manchester. The Royal Exchange staged his first two professional plays, *Cannibals* and *Single Sex*, along with his translation of Anton Chekhov's *The Cherry Orchard*. His other original plays include *Mates in Chelsea, Pity, Saint George and the Dragon, The Wolf from the Door, Each Slow Dusk* and *The Grandfathers*. He has also translated *Three Sisters* and *The Oresteia* for Shakespeare's Globe and *Remembrance Day* for the Royal Court, and written the libretti for three operas: *The Skating Rink, Coraline* and *The Way Back Home*. Rory's work has won him a Pearson bursary for the Royal Exchange, the Harold Pinter Commission for the Royal Court, the James Tait Black Prize for Drama, and co-won him the Abraham Woursell Prize and the George Devine Award for Most Promising Playwright.

James Macdonald – Director

James was an Associate Director of the Royal Exchange in the early 1990s, directing *Loves Labours Lost* and *Richard III* – both starring Linus Roache. These days he is mostly directs new plays. He was an Associate at the Royal Court for 14 years, and has directed 28 world premiere productions there, including Rory Mullarkey's *Wolf from the Door*. He has worked for almost all of the other major new writing theatres in London and New York. A number of these productions have transferred to the West End and Broadway, where he has also directed classic plays by Edward Albee, Tennessee Williams, Sam Shepard – and recently Samuel Beckett's *Waiting for Godot*. He has collaborated most frequently with the playwrights Caryl Churchill, Sarah Kane, Annie Baker, Mike Bartlett, Lucy Kirkwood, Sam Grabiner and Martin Crimp.

Laura Hopkins – Designer

Laura is an award-winning set and costume designer, working throughout the UK and internationally in theatre, opera, dance and experimental performance. Theatre designs include: *Legally Blonde* (Regent's Park Open Air Theatre); *Rockets and Blue Lights* (National Theatre); *Dracula, Night of the Living Dead* (Imitating the Dog); *One for Sorrow, The Pass* (Royal Court); *The Divide* (EIF/Old Vic); *Troilus & Cressida* (The Wooster Group/RSC); *Falstaff* (ENO/Opera North); *The Seagull* (Headlong); *Black Watch* (NTS); *The Golden Ass* (Shakespeare's Globe). Awards include: UK Theatre Award for Best Design *(Dracula)*; Critics' Awards for Theatre in Scotland Award for Best Design *(Lanark)*; TMA Awards for Best Design *(Doctor Faustus* and *Mister Heracles)*. She is an associate artist with Imitating the Dog theatre company and Duckie, Purveyors of Progressive Working Class Entertainment. Since 2018 she has been developing her own politically engaged performance work combining formal experiment with popular entertainment.

Charles Balfour – Lighting Designer

Previously at the Royal Exchange Theatre: *The Suppliant Women, The Accrington Pals, Orlando, To Kill a Mockingbird, Good.* Recent work includes *The Holy Rosenbergs* (Menier Chocolate Factory); *Endgame* (Ustinov Bath); *Ben and Imo, Here In America* (Orange Tree); *The Three Musketeers* (New Vic); *Get Up Stand Up: The Bob*

Marley Story (West End). Other theatre includes *The Corn Is Green,
Ma Rainey's Black Bottom* (National Theatre); *The River* (Broadway);
*Romeo and Juliet, The Alchemist, Queen Anne, A Midsummer Night's
Dream* (RSC); *Who's Afraid of Virginia Woolf, Richard III, Mojo, Posh*
(West End); *The Kite Runner* (West End, Broadway & tour); *The Prime
of Miss Jean Brodie* (Donmar); *The Events* (Young Vic/New York
Theater Workshop); *Choir Boy, Chicken Soup with Barley, The Ugly
One* (Royal Court); *The Beauty Queen of Leenane* (Young Vic); *Our
Lady of Kibeho* (Northampton Royal). Charles also has many UK and
international credits in dance and opera since 1986.

Ian Dickinson – Sound Designer

Ian started his theatre career at the Royal Exchange Theatre. Theatre
credits include: *Fatherland, Mogadishu, 1984, Macbeth, Port, Poor
Superman, Fast Food and Coyote Ugly* (Royal Exchange Theatre);
Les Liaisons Dangereuses (National Theatre); *The Battle* (The Rep);
Unfortunate (The Lowry); *The Hunger Games* (Troubadour Canary
Wharf); *Hedda* (Ustinov Studio); *Fear of 13* (Donmar); *Waiting For
Godot* (Haymarket Theatre Royal); *Alma Mater* (Almeida); *The
Witches* (National Theatre); *Boys On The Verge Of Tears* (Soho
Theatre); *2:22 A Ghost Story* (West End, Los Angeles & UK Tour); *The
Ocean At The End Of The Lane* (UK Tour & Duke of York's); *A
Midsummer Night's Dream* (Shakespeare North Playhouse); *Angels
in America* (Broadway). Ian was the recipient of both Olivier and
Drama Desk awards for *The Curious Incident of the Dog in the
Nighttime*, which played at the National Theatre and subsequently
toured venues worldwide.

Georgina Lamb – Movement And Intimacy Director

Georgina is a director, choreographer and movement director. She is
an original member of Frantic Assembly. Recent theatre includes:
Shadowlands (West End); *Sherlock Holmes and the Twelve Days of
Christmas* (Birmingham Rep); *The Last 5 Years* (UK Tour); *The Great
British Bake Off the Musical* (West End); *Much Ado About Nothing*
(The Globe); *A Christmas Carol, Titus Andronicus, Roaring Girl,
Romeo and Juliet* (RSC); *A Christmas Carol* (Nottingham Playhouse/
Alexandra Palace); *Piaf* (Nottingham Playhouse); *Assassins*
(Nottingham Playhouse/Watermill Theatre); *Shadowlands, The
Midnight Gang, A Christmas Carol, Grimm Tales, The Witches,
Running Wild* (Chichester Festival Theatre); *Macbeth* (Chichester

Festival Theatre/West End/New York); *Frozen, Much Ado About Nothing* (West End); *Chimerica* (Almeida/West End); *Sweeney Todd* (West End/New York). Television and film credits include: *Juice* (VAL/BBC), *Hansel and Gretel* (BBC/Lambent. BAFTA & BANFF Winner); *True Stories* (BBC); *Once Upon a Time* (BBC/Lambent); *Macbeth* (Illuminations media).

Amy Ball CDG – Casting Director

Theatre includes: *1536* (Almeida/Ambassadors); *The Weir* (Harold Pinter); *Small Hotel* (Theatre Royal Bath); *Mrs Warren's Profession* (Garrick); *The Hunger Games* (Troubadour); *The Years* (Almeida/Harold Pinter); *Unicorn* (Garrick); *Slave Play* (Noel Coward); *The Hills of California* (Harold Pinter); *Jerusalem* (Apollo); *Leopoldstadt* (Wyndham's); *Uncle Vanya* (Harold Pinter Theatre); *The Son* (Duke of York's/Kiln Theatre); *The Night of the Iguana* (Noël Coward Theatre); *Sweat* (Gielgud/Donmar Warehouse); *Rosmersholm* (Duke of York's); *True West* (Vaudeville); *The Ferryman* (Royal Court/Gielgud/Bernard B. Jacobs Theatre); *The Moderate Soprano* (Hampstead/Duke of York's); *The Birthday Party, Who's Afraid of Virginia Woolf?* (Harold Pinter Theatre); *Consent* (National Theatre/Harold Pinter Theatre); *The Goat, or Who is Sylvia?* (Theatre Royal Haymarket); *Hangmen* (Royal Court/Wyndham's/Atlantic Theatre Company); *A Doll's House, Christmas Day, Romans, Women Beware the Devil, Daddy, The Hunt, Shipwreck, Dance Nation, Albion* (Almeida); *Paradise, Stories, Exit the King* (National Theatre); *White Noise, A Very Very Very Dark Matter* (Bridge Theatre).

Keston & Keston – Childrens' Casting Director

Theatre credits: *The Greatest Showman* (World Premiere, Bristol Hippodrome); *The Lion King* (Lyceum Theatre, West End); *Inter Alia* (Wyndham's Theatre, West End); *Atlantis* (Theatr Clwyd/Chichester Festival Theatre); *The Sound of Music* (Opera North); *A Knight's Tale* (World Premiere, Manchester Opera House); *13 Going on 30 The Musical* (World Premiere Manchester Opera); *Freaky Friday* (UK Premiere); *Charlie and the Chocolate Factory* (UK & Ireland Tour/Leeds Playhouse); *A Christmas Carol* (Leeds Playhouse); *Oliver!* (Leeds Playhouse); *Nativity! The Musical* (London/Birmingham Rep/UK Tour); *Winnie the Pooh* (UK Premiere & UK Tour); *Bonnie & Clyde* (Arts Theatre, West End/Theatre Royal Drury Lane); *The Children's Inquiry* (LUNG/Southwark Playhouse); *How the Grinch Stole

Christmas (UK Premiere/UK Tour). Film credits: *Christmas on Mistletoe Farm* (Netflix). Television credits: *The Grinch Live!* (NBC/Universal); *Secret Invasion* (Marvel).

Emily McLaughlin – Dramaturg

Emily is New Work Consultant at the Royal Exchange Theatre and a freelance dramaturg, script executive and creative consultant working across stage and screen. She was previously Head of Development at Fictionhouse, and the founding Head of New Work at the National Theatre, where she established and led the New Work department, overseeing both the Literary team and the NT Studio. At the National Theatre, she commissioned, developed and creatively produced numerous award-winning new plays across all three stages, with extended life in the West End and on screen via NT Live, NT at Home and Sky Arts. Prior to this, she was Artistic Associate at the Royal Court Theatre, where she worked over twelve years with three successive Artistic Directors to discover and support a new generation of playwrights. She is a Trustee of the Lyric Hammersmith Theatre.

Katie Greenall – Associate Director

Katie (she/they) is a director, theatre maker and writer. She specialises in new writing, solo autobiographical work and working with Young People and Communities. She is currently the Associate Director (Creative Exchange) at the Royal Exchange Theatre. Previously she was the Associate Director at the Bush Theatre, where she established the Bush Young Companies. Directing credits include: *Heart Wall*, *Make Me Feel*, *Communion* (Bush Theatre); *We All Know How This Ends* (Theatre Royal Stratford East); *As We Face The Sun* (Offie Nominated, Bush Theatre); *Pass It On* (Bush Theatre); *Here, Here, Here* (Theatre Royal Stratford East); *Anthem* (Bush Theatre); *Back Up!* (Bush Theatre). She was also the Associate Director on *Barcelona* (Duke of York's Theatre).

Sadie Mears – Birkbeck Assistant Director

Sadie is currently training on the Birkbeck Theatre Directing MFA and is on secondment as the Resident Birkbeck Trainee Director at the Royal Exchange Theatre. Her credits as Assistant Director include: *Private Lives, Road, Singin' in the Rain* (Royal Exchange Theatre);

Dancing at Laughnasa (Royal Exchange Theatre and Sheffield Theatre); *Revolt. She Said. Revolt Again.* (Rose Bruford). Credits as director include: *The Beauty Queen of Leenane* (The Pegg Studio Theatre, Bristol); *Strapped* (The Island, Bristol); *Party Time* (Extinction Rebellion, Southeast London Festival). Credits as associate include: *Clean Slate* (Summerhall and Riverside Bitesize Festival).

For this Production

Naomi Albans Chaperone
Ed Aylward Chaperone
Tabitha Bowman Chaperone
Andy Bubble Set Builder
Cat Cameron Wigs Hair and Make-up Assistant
Dave Chesters Stage Technician
Dave Clare Stage Technician
Ben Cook Workshop Manager
Siobhan Distion Dresser
Izzy Farrar Chaperone
Annabeth Fernley Milliner
Laura Ford Chaperone
Tom Giovanni Scenic Artist
Dean Michael Gregory Stage Technician
Brian Hanlon Prop Maker
Katrina Heath Chaperone
Beth Kynaston Dresser
Lily Makinson Costume Assistant
Helen Masters Wigs Hair and Make-up Supervisor
Anne-Marie McNab Chaperone
Nikki Meredith Costume Supervisor
Angela Merino Chaperone
Ellie Nicholas Costume Assistant
Simon Pemberton Set Builder
Ella Roberts Chaperone
Helen Simmons Voice Coach
Sam Stedman Stage Technician
Margaret Walsh Chaperone
Carly Wedge Chaperone
Tristian Willis Automation Operator
Sarah Worrall Prop Maker

Community Cast

Jada Adewale
Sophia Aiello
Heritage Awesanya
Willem Babrovskie
Gemma Barrington
Gill Bassam
Steve Bassam
Ettie Bennett
Colin Blackledge
Nathan Bradley
Marcus Bradshaw
Ellen Breheny
Belle Brien
Melanie Broughton
Chloe Buckley
Nick Burke
Elizabeth Cameron
Rob Caudwell
Simeon Caudwell
Cherry Chan
Cyrus Choy
Levinia Clemeston
Heather Cole
Ellie Cordwell
Ophelia Cordwell
Evan Cunliffe
Tom Cunningham
Konde Dauda
Ivan Davis
Mark Dawson
Brendan Delphinius-Lopez
Milly Doregos
Isabelle Dorrian
Harriet Eaton
Elaine Fell
Paul Foster
Damian Frendo
Catherine Fyfe
Stephen Garratt
Chloe Gorrod
Dave Gorvett
Paul Green
Stephen Hall
Finch Hamil
Charlie Hill
Anthony Houghton
Victoria Hoyle
Nicole Iwobi
River Kerr
Noa Kidane
Esther Kimani
Ryan Kinsi
Jack Kirkpatrick
Helen Kozak
Kayden Lai
Stephen Lee
Zheng Yuan Lee
Olivia Leishman
Ava Lewis-Vasco
Nathaniel Lewis-Vasco
Annabelle Lloyd Hughes
Joanne Lowndes
Emer Mac Manus
Jane Martin
Doretta LorraineMaynard
Yuan McCabe
Peter McKinney
Thomas McLeish
Beya Milan
Peter Mungovan
Eve Njoroge
Victoria Okhiria
Jayran Oskoei-Lear
Myra Pennington
Emmy Quall
Stewart Racle
Tina Ramos Ekongo
Tabitha Reid
Marlies Reisch-Gallagher
Rebecca Riley

Freddie Rimmer
Terry Robinson
Patricia Russell
Abosede Sanusi-Shoga
Ann Sarge
Reggie Shirley
Eira Short
Paula Simbu
Sofia Skorytska
Tilly Spencer
Harry Spooner
Ethan Stringer
Steven Szoltysek
Emmeline Thomas
Rosie Thomas
Ez Thompson
Lenny Tunnicliffe
Anthony Walsh
Aaron Watts
David Weston
Lucy Weston
Opal Weston
Jennifer Wightman
Emily Williams
Robin Wright

Choirs

St Philips CofE Primary School, Salford
Razzamataz Theatre Schools Manchester South
Kitty Watson Academy of Performing Arts Manchester
Shooting Star Theatre School Manchester
Footlights Theatre Manchester

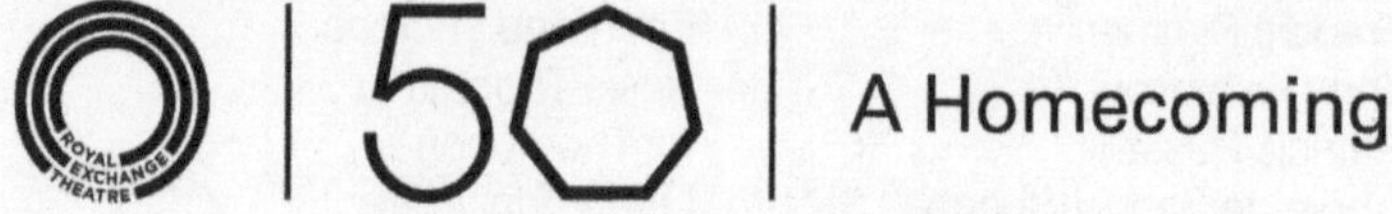

About the Royal Exchange Theatre

Manchester's Royal Exchange Theatre Company transforms the way people see theatre, each other and the world around them. Our historic building, once the world's biggest cotton exchange, was taken over by artists in 1976. Today it is an award-winning cultural charity that produces new theatre in-the-round, in communities, on the road and online.

Exchange remains at the heart of everything we make and do. Our currency is brand new drama and reinvigorated classics, the boldest artists and a company of highly skilled makers – all brought together in an imaginative endeavour to share ideas and experiences with the people of Greater Manchester (and beyond).

The Exchange's unique auditorium is powerfully democratic, a space where audiences and performers meet as equals, entering and exiting through the same doors. It is the inspiration for all we do; inviting everyone to understand the past, engage in today's big questions, collectively imagine a better future and lose themselves in the moment of a great night out.

In 2026 our iconic theatre celebrates 50 years of producing award-winning plays, creating work that is ambitious in ideas, form and scale right in the heart of Manchester's city centre.

royalexchange.co.uk

Executive

Artistic Director/Co-CEO **Selina Cartmell**
Executive Director/Co-CEO **Sheena Wrigley**

Registered Charity No. 255424. To donate and find out more visit:
//royalexchange.co.uk/supportus

Marketing
Natalie Forrester Head of Marketing
Zahra Iqbal Marketing Officer
Thomas McCormack Marketing & Content Manager
Liam Steers Digital Content Producer
Wesley Thistlethwaite Director of Audiences & Visitor Experience
Vicky Wormald CRM & Audiences Data Manager

Operations
Matthew Clifford Facilities Manager
Christiaan de Villiers Director of Buildings & Facilities
Grace Sadiku IT Technician

Cleaning Contractors
Mavis Asantewan, Sue Borough, Elaine Connolly, Linda Egbon,
Moussa Kouyate, Solomon Onajnfe, Ewa Opala, Malgorzata Pagiela,
Karolina Sawczuk

Hospitality & Events
Caitlin Conners Head of Commercial, Hospitality and Events
Vistie James Duty Manager (casual)
Sean Maher Events & Hospitality Manager
Vistie Marsden Events Coordinator
Lydia Trench Kitchen Assistant

Production
Simon Curtis Production Support
Mark Distin-Webster Head of Lighting
Rachael Duncan Jones Costume Maintenance
Tracy Dunk Head of Costume
Bridget Fell Running Wardrobe Lead
Helen Hall Production Manager
Rosie Holditch Costume Assistant
Felicia Jagne Deputy Head of Costume
Kevin Leach Head of Technical Stage
Matt Lever Head of Lighting
Matthew Masson Head of Sound
Max Schule Sound Technician
Joanna Shepstone Head of Wigs Hair & Makeup
Tom Sutcliffe Lighting Senior
Antony Walters Deputy Head of Technical Stage
Sarah White Costume Cutter & Maker
Lucy Woodcock Costume Hire Facilitator

The Rivals Team

Events and Hospitality Manager
Sean Maher

Kitchen Assistant
Lydia Trench

Hospitality Supervisors
Jessica Gale
Joe Hodgson
Aaron Shaw
Helen Thomason
Lois Mackie

Hospitality Assistants
Vicky Absolon
Jmelia Braithwaite
Penelope Bunyan
Stella Cohen
Molly Crighton
Tsen Day-Beaver
Lewis Eades
Lauren Ellis-Stretch
Georgia Hathaway
Ariel Hebditch
Sedge James
Josie Julyan
Zofia Komorowska
Lola Middleton
Ashley O'Brien
Beata Potrzebowski
Kacper Potrzebowski
Grace Pullin
Julia Rogers
Gareth Smith
Katy Smith
Lydia Trench
Rose Warburton
Rachel Zanetti

Security Contractors
Fawad Ali Khan, Olufemi Shangobyi, Atif Riaz

Visitor Experience
Matt Averall Stage Door Coordinator
Rachel Davies Box Office & Memberships Manager
Sophie Edmunds Visitor Experience Supervisor
Eleanor Harrington Duty Manager (casual)
Maisie Holland Duty Manager (casual)
Jennifer Hulman Box Office & Memberships Supervisor
Niah Mandla Stage Door Coordinator
Katie Merrick Stage Door Coordinator
Camille Philardeau Duty Manager (Casual)
Mike Seal Visitor Experience Manager
Matthew Warren Duty Manager (casual) & Box Office &
Memberships Supervisor

Visitor Experience Coordinators: Clodagh Chapman, Molly
Crighton, Amelia Cox, Eleanor Harrington, Maisie Holland, Vistie
Marsden, Ren Roberts, Holly Simpson

Visitor Experience Assistants: Linnae Abraham, Vicky Absolon,
Richard Barry, Anusia Battersby, Lauren Billingsley, Emma Bourke,
Katy Brooks, Rachel Burbridge, Jasmine Burt, Hamish Campbell-
Colquhoun, Clodagh Chapman, Iona Chisholm, Mika Cholewa, Julie
Anne Cowan, Amelia Cox, Molly Crighton, Ishita Daas, Tsen Day-
Beaver, Maya Dhokia, Natasha Dutton, Nia Edwards, Aimee
Eggington, Lily Farrow, Neil Geddes, Alicia Glasgow, Chloe Gorrod,
Ashley Gregory, Eleanor Harrington, Richard Harrison, Amelia Hall,
Ioana Hayder, William Hayes, Katrina Heath, Ariel Hebditch, Jenny
Hill, Maisie Holland, Rebecca Johnson, Megan Jones, Fernanda
Juarez-Vazquez, Josie Julyan, Paul Kirkman, Waleria Koba, Ella
Laughton, Nai-Kong Leung, Isobel Liddle, Benjamin Lucas, Sadie
Mears, Chris McKiernon, Alistair McNicol, Jacqui McPeake, Phoebe
Mycroft, Tony O'Driscoll, Chris Owen, Camille Philardeau, Emilee
Prince, Xsara-Sheneille Pryce, Ren Roberts, Adam Rogers, Julia
Rogers, Ethan Scott, Ayshea Shames, Holly Simpson, Marta
Szadowska, Candace Tai, Jess Telling, Helen Thomason, Jess
Timperley, Anna Vasey, Rose Warburton, Matthew Warren, Esme
Watts, Anna Whittle, Eliott Whittle, Beth Whooly, Joseph Woolf,
Mahdi Zadeh

Volunteers
David Akinola, Nigel J Anderson, Emaan asif, Carol Barber, Richard
Barlow, Tracy Barlow, Suzanne Batty, David Black, Deborah Bhatti,
Ste Borg, Gill Borkin, Arnold Bradshaw, Chris Brown, Julie Campbell,
Kathryn Cant, Jim Capewell, Jose Caramelo, Jill Cavan, Jiaqi Chen,

Gary Cohen, Grace Collier, Jackie Corr, Calise Cottriall, Gill Davies, Xinzi Deng, Pat Dexter, Heather Doona, Christine Duffin, Anne Thor Dupont, Aimee Eggington, Hollie Fabola, Barbara Feddy, Anna Fiske, Kam Ki Fong, Irene Gray, Ron Goodier, Chloe Gordon, Nigel Gratton, Annie Guo, Sarah Halliday, Paul Harper, Tori Harris-Burton, Carolyn Harrison, Laura Hawgood, John Hilton, Louise Hill, Yvonne Hindle, Elaine Patricia Houlden, Matt Hudson, Alison Johnston, Peter Jones, Kseniia Karpovskaia, Iffat Kauser, Lee Keen, Paul Kirkman, Kashish Kotecha, Talal Kurdi, Oluwabukola Lebi, Isobel Liddle, Sheila Lowe, Stella Lowe, Swetha Mamidi, Janet McFarland, Linda McLoughlin, Celine McNally, Jane Marlow, Salma Mehboob, Lewis Montgomery, Peter Mungovan, Hilary Murray, Ruquayyah Othman, Christine Ovens, Clare Marie Papali, George Parker-Conway, Jack Parkin, Myra Pennington, Tomas Petr, Hilary Poole, Tony Pounder, Anne Reeves, Helen Roberts, Simon Robison, Ana Rojas, Jean Ross, Icadel Ryan, Stephanie Rylance, Eisuke Sato, Ethan Scott, Maurice Shaw, Richard Simpson, Jenna Spray, Deborah Stephenson, Pete Stephenson, Annie-Rose Surigao, Celine Tandiono, Momo Tanimomo, Jo Taylor, Louis Giles Thompson, Yvonne Trace, Charlie Veitch, Olivia Waite, Charley Wakefield, Val Wallwork, Isabel Watson, Mike White, Tonia Williams, Xueting Zhang, Shenqian Zhong

Honorary Associates
Paul Lee (Chairman 1999–2015)
Ben Caldwell (Chairman 2015–2023)
Armoghan Mohammed (Chairman 2023–2025)

The Royal Exchange Theatre has been bringing the world's most powerful stories to life for 50 years. As a registered charity, we rely on the generous support of individuals, businesses and charitable trusts to help us continue to create extraordinary theatre on our stage and in our communities.

There are a number of ways that you can support the Royal Exchange Theatre, to find out more on how you can get involved please contact us.
Email donations@royalexchange.co.uk

Principal Funders
Arts Council England
GMCA (Greater Manchester
Combined Authority)
The Oglesbey Charitable Trust

Corporate Partner
Bruntwood

Corporate Sponsor
Levitt Bernstein
Edwardian Hotels
Fumo by San Carlo
Galloways Printers
King Street Townhouse
Royal Exchange Flowers Ltd
The Cut & Craft
Stock Exchange Hotel

Principal Corporate Member
Edmundson Electrical

Encore Corporate Member
Beyond Corporate Law
Mills & Reeve
Ralli Solicitors LLP
Sanderson Weatherall

Associate Corporate Member
5plus Architects
Hotel Indigo
Specsavers Manchester Arndale

Supporters' Circle
Rachel Armstrong
Jason Austin
Meg & Peter Cooper
John & Penny Early

Mike Edge & Pippa England
Stephen & Sarah Edmondson
Stephen Garratt
Rachel Haugh
Richard & Elaine Johnson
Carole Nash OBE
Nicola Shindler

Platinum Members
Stuart Bishop
Colin Blackledge
Mr J Bishop & Mr J Taylor
Sir Robert & Dr Meriel Boyd
Angela Brookes
Paul & Ann Cannings
Sarah Davnall
Mrs V Fletcher
Peter & Judy Folkman
Irene Gray
Roy & Maria Greenwood
Ellen Hanlon
Michael & Kerrith Harris
Simon & Katherine Johnson
Stephen & Arlene Moss
Stephen & Judy Poster
Robin & Mary Taylor
Helen & Phil Wiles
Gold Members
Daniel Bohuslaw
Dan Byrne & Helena Torre Sevillano
Bill Connor
John & Kim Fox
Geoff Holman
Jacquie Long
Stella Lowe
Donald Mather

Even These Things

Notes

This play is in three parts.

Part One *is a monologue.*

Part Two *is a kind of procession.*

Part Three *most resembles a conventional play.*

But stage them however you like . . .

Part One

Pig Annie

Place: Angel Meadow, Manchester.

Time: Sunday, 14 June 1846.

Cast

Annie Donovan – a woman from the West of Ireland

This play is a monologue, but the interjections may be performed by other actors.

The tempo throughout is fast.

Annie   Elizabeth Crosby murdered my pig so I'm going to beat her to death

The fight's to take place at four o'the clock on this the fourteenth day of June in The Year of Our Lord Eighteen Forty-Six at St Michael's Flags Angel Meadow Manchester and there's only one rule

No tummy-shots

So you can all come if you like or don't I don't give a fuck what you do Lizzie Crosby's getting beaten to death for murdering my pig either way

Oh she was a fine pig my pig pink as a fresh summer rose downy blond hair all over her back a ring that was my deceased mother's in her soft left ear and she was called Annie just like me

Most folk thought it strange I named my pig after myself they assumed there'd be continual confusion when it came to the attracting of attention but I assure you there was little confusion after all I'd hardly have need to attract my own attention so it was clear when I shouted for Annie I must be referring to the pig and the pig could hardly have shouted for me being as she was a pig and so the only circumstance under which confusion might have arisen would have been one where there was a third party involved although confusion here could usually be avoided by a correct understanding of the context for instance the injunction "Annie stop chewing that curtain" was most probably directed towards the pig although I have been known to chew a curtain from time to time or by the judicious use of hand gestures to the extent that confusion over which Annie was being referred to occurred at the most a dozen times in her short and very beautiful life

I had her off a Moroccan in Smithfield Market who'd come into possession of a litter of piglets by one nefarious means or another and now was keen to be rid of them on account of his religion forbidding too much contact with such animals and since that day in the market we'd been inseparable she'd been my solace in the daytime and my warmth in the night and when she laughed because she did laugh that pig it was almost a human laugh ringing in the air she was all that was good in the world Pig Annie and now she's gone thanks to the murderous appetite of one Lizzie Crosby who'll get her payment this very afternoon

But before I kill Lizzie Crosby I must first excite my courage by having sex with a handsome Yorkshireman called Marcus

"What's the matter Annie" says the handsome Yorkshireman called Marcus when he's finished having sex with me "Are you thinking about Virgil's epic poem *The Aeneid* again"

Although this may seem a surprising question it is in fact a sign of Marcus's deep knowledge of my character that he knew my deceased father was a schoolmaster in Dunmore who drew out the entire form of his existence as one long quotation from Golden Age Roman authors meaning that I myself was drowned in Latin poetry growing up and if I were ever to be gazing morosely into the middle-distance I probably was indeed thinking about Virgil's epic poem *The Aeneid*

On this occasion however I am not

"No of course I'm not thinking about Virgil's epic poem *The Aeneid* Marcus you fucking moron" I call him the latter to deflect from how touched I feel about the obvious attention he's paid to absorbing my personal history

"I was thinking" I say "About Pig Annie about her laugh that was almost a human laugh and about how that's stopped now because Lizzie Crosby pulped her vocal cords to put into a soup for herself and her revolting elderly husband"

Lizzie Crosby's husband is almost literally fossilised a prehistoric fellow and no joke

"Well I've been thinking Annie" says Marcus "that I don't think you should fight her"

"You fucking what Marcus" I say

"I don't think you should fight her" says he

"Does the principle of retributive justice mean nothing to you Marcus" says I "does the age-old *lex talionis* hold no sway in your soft Huddersfield heart that bitch murdered Pig Annie Marcus and when she did it wasn't just an animal she killed it was my very other self she put from the Earth so I won't rest till the dark ground of St Michael's drinks down her murdering blood and Pig Annie's soft pink ghost can finally sleep avenged"

"I understand that you're upset about your pig Annie" says Marcus

"It's not just the pig Marcus" says I "It's the whole heap of injuries piled upon me by the various scions of the Crosby family that Lizzie thinks she's so much better than me with her fake Ancoats accent even though I know for a fact she's actually from Donegal and her husband's sailor's pension which given his superannuated condition was probably bestowed on him around the time of the Spanish Armada and her multiple miscreant infants who laugh at me for selling matches and living in a cellar and having no food all the time"

"That reminds me" says Marcus "Do you want some food"

"Yes please I haven't eaten for three days" I say so he takes the kettle off the stove and pours some hot water over a chicken bone and gives it to me

I chew the wet bone and pretend not to cry for a bit

"I'm saying I don't think you should fight" says Marcus "On account of your condition"

There are multiple things he could be referring to here but I assume in this instance he means the fact that I'm currently seven months pregnant with his child

"If you're implying Marcus" I say softly after a brief silence "that women-with-child shouldn't engage in strenuous physical activity I suggest you take yourself over the other side of the Irwell to the workhouse and make your complaint to the pregnant inmates there or to the pregnant piecers in Arkwright's mill why just last week I saw three female Chartists each one of them heavy with triplets set fire to a factory before sitting down in the street holding hands and giving birth simultaneously to their combined total of nine babies not half an hour later"

"I'm doubtful that happened" says Marcus

"And didn't you yourself just engage in acts worthy of a travelling troupe of sexual acrobats with a female more than seven months gone"

"I fear for the little one's safety is all" he says

"Might I then draw your attention to the only rule of the bout" says I

"No tummy-shots"

"I fear for your safety too"

"If you feared that much you'd have married me by now" says I

"I'm still saving up for a ring" says he

"I had a perfectly good ring" I say "it was my dear departed mother's put into my hand by the woman herself just minutes before she died and subsequently snipped and put in Pig Annie's ear before that murdering thief Lizzie Crosby took it and probably pawned it to buy more fake Manchester accent lessons now you watch my lips as I say this Marcus *di talia Grais instaurate pio si poenas ore reposco* that's from Virgil's epic poem *The Aeneid* you cunt and it means don't you dare stand in the way of my vengeance or I'll boot your skinny arse all the way back over the Pennines" and then I walk out slamming the flimsy door behind me

My courage hardly excited by this exchange I leave the cramped second-floor bunkroom Marcus shares with eleven other similarly handsome Yorkshire furnace-stokers on Back Old Mount Street descend the rotting staircase and step out into the bright Sunday afternoon sunshine

The stagnant Irk's there green and bubbling and stinking of bubonic armpits like an English river Styx and the hodgepodge houses crowd out the light as I step over the various recumbent bodies of Scotsmen and Austrians still snoozing away after Saturday night's drinking the streaks of vomit on the corners of their sleeping mouths and all over their tatty trousers combine with the general stench of the fetid air to create an atmosphere I can only describe as fucking horrible

I turn to head back to my cellar

"Good afternoon to you Miss Donovan"

Oh shit it's Father Hearne probably here to admonish me for not going to mass

"I was wondering if you might sell me some matches"

Thank fuck for that though I suppose he'd know better than to try to get me over to Saint Patrick's given my often-vocalised view that no benevolent creator could possibly have fashioned a landscape so covered in faeces and besides it's a bit of a walk to that church

"How many you want"

"Just a sixpence worth will that buy me a box"

"It'll buy you two boxes or one box and a short window of time in which to harangue me about something or other"

"I'll take the latter then"

"I thought you might say that" I say as I chuck him the box of matches and he hands me a shiny silver sixpence which I try to grab nonchalantly and without letting him know that my mouth's already started watering

"Do you like the world Annie Donovan" he says beaming smugly as if that's the best fucking question anyone's ever asked

"I hate the world Father Hearne" I say "It's the worst place I've ever been"

"The worst place you've ever been Annie Donovan now is that quite the attitude in which to bring fresh new life hither I ask you"

"If this is about your fearing for my safety in my upcoming set-to with Elizabeth Crosby Father then let me tell you I've had quite enough of sententious men telling me who I can or cannot fight to the death for one Sunday afternoon thank you very much"

"Oh I have no fear for your safety Annie I'm well aware that you'll flatten the girl and in my non-ecumenical capacity I thoroughly hope that you do however the last I checked murder or the attempt thereof was a transportational offence and if you think the rats in Angel Meadow are bad they've spiders the size of small dogs to contend with down there in Van Diemen's Land"

"Well maybe I like big spiders Father"

"You're a bright girl Annie you came over last year didn't you"

I choose not to answer this question

"I can't imagine how it must feel to lose your family and everyone you know like that"

Does this prick not understand the concept of a deafening silence

"But we're all here together now Annie and we're building this place and we'd be sad to see you leave it"

"*Una salus victis nullam sperare salutem* Father" I say as I turn and snatch my skirts out of a pile of horse manure I didn't realise was there "The only hope for the vanquished is to have no hope at all enjoy your matches"

And I'm gone with the sun in my face and the priest gazing pensively after me I'm gone now with but half an hour to go till the fight and a nice shiny sixpence warm in my trembling hand

A sixpence a sixpence the day belongs to me all Manchester is mine from the market to the river the mills are mine and the shit-strewn streets the whole city's a stage for the performance of my largesse and the Tyrolese oompah band that plays on the corner of Ludgate Hill this afternoon plays only for Annie Donovan play boys play blow the brass fearless and bright watch the wealthy lady dance and teach me how to spend my untold riches

She dances.

Oh perchance I'll buy an apple or two apples or one apple and two plums or one plum and two apples or one apple and a fig oh a fig just for me a fig on some bread with a little bit of butter fill me right up for the fight oh maybe some lard a rasher of bacon some salt can you imagine a pinch of salt just for me or dried fruit oh soft dried apricots little golden suns like a I'm duchess or something or maybe three plums and nothing else or two plums and an apple or one plum one apple one fig oh the decisions the decisions the glorious fabulous decisions but of course I've immediately gone to the pub instead

There's no Irish allowed right now in St Michael's Tavern or in The Angel or ironically enough in the Exile of Erin and there's very specifically no Annie Donovans allowed in The Old Victory due to a misunderstanding involving the pickled egg jar and the landlady's glass eye and the same goes for The Duke of Connaught I should really stop attempting that magic trick in the pub but at least The Dog and Duck's always open to all so that's where I head and neck the biggest gin they'll give me and now the sixpence is gone

Do you judge me gentlefolk

Do you sit in the safety of your comfortable chairs and think you wouldn't do the very same as me

There's a sensation just after the gin goes down it's a warm sensation that starts at the back of your throat then moves up to your head and down to your heart as it blooms and blooms in your blood it's a sensation that feels like forgetfulness it's a sensation that feels like love and if you lived my life if you spent my time if your eyes were mine and you'd seen what I'd seen with them you wouldn't judge me that sensation my friends no not for a universe of apricots

I stand in that sensation

I'd live there forever if I could

And The Duck's rammed as usual with all of the regulars in the thieves laying silver cigarette cases on the table and glancing about for detectives the organ grinder grinding a sorrowful waltz in the corner the Lithuanian man who's forced his pet bear-cub to wear a little boy's funeral suit for some reason and German Fred propping up the bar with his pint and his notebook as ever

"You alright there German Fred" I say

"Hello Miss Annie" he says and takes a big sip "And where is your porcine companion today"

I'd sometimes bring Pig Annie down The Duck when she was alive and German Fred would feed her rusks it almost makes me sob to think of it

"She's currently spread piecemeal among the stomachs of a fake English washerwoman named Elizabeth Crosby and her reprobate family who killed her for the dual purpose of satisfying their hunger and of making me very sad" I say

"Well I am sorry to hear that" says Fred "She was a good pig"

"She was" I say

The slow waltz continues

"I'm actually about to head over to Saint Michael's Flags to beat her to death you can come if you like or don't I don't give a fuck what you do"

"Ah the weekly Sunday bare-knuckle matches I was told there'd be females contending today I suppose it was only a matter of time before you took part"

"What's that supposed to mean" I say gruffly

"Pigs and fighting Miss Annie the Irish obsessions" he smiles and taps on his notebook

"Well for starters you prick my pig was Moroccan and for seconds I've lived three decades now on this godforsaken planet and I never saw an Irishman punch another before I came to Manchester"

"Do you mean to suggest Miss Annie" he says licking his thumb with his long German tongue and wetting the end of his pen "that the causes of violent events stem less from the aggressor's innate national characteristics and more from their historical and material circumstances because if you do my next volume may require some annotations"

"I mean to suggest that if you cram thirty thousand of us into a space barely big enough to breathe in you'd forgive us if it sharpens our elbows a little now if you'll excuse me German Fred I'm due to see a woman about a pig"

The smell of the street hits me before the sunlight does a whole year here now and I've still never got used to it shit *(sniffs)* and vomit *(sniffs)* and smoke *(sniffs)* and sweat *(sniffs)* and biscuits *(sniffs)* and somebody's burning hair *(sniffs)* some of the regulars know where I'm headed so they follow me variously limping and burping and lurching and dancing as

the tipsy procession heads down the hill to the back of the
station gathering more prospective audience from among
the beggars and the doorway-sleepers as we go

A man outside Gibraltar's playing *The Black Velvet Band* badly
on a tin whistle a group of Chartists stand and chant for
better hours holding their elaborate signs give it a rest lads
it's Sunday and I'm feeling it now the courage rise a little the
gin's set about its trustworthy job and here's the black glass
of Victoria Station yawning and spewing out fresh loads of
human livestock from Liverpool and the boats beyond
tremblers gazing about with old-country knapsacks and
confusion hollow cheeks still red from the wind on the sea
ready to begin their new lives welcome to Manchester boys
abandon hope all ye who fucking enter here

And we're up to the Red Bank now where the Polish and the
Africans who keep themselves to themselves gaze rigidly at
their month-old newspapers as we pass while the womenfolk
step back from the window-frames and only the small
children crane their necks and stare the little one inside me
gives a kick to say hello and I place my hand on the place
where the kick comes and try not to think as we cross the
green river Irk that bubbles and spits and reach St Michael's
Flags at last

The previous fight's still in progress as we arrive a Russian
and a Prussian swing wearily at one another in the centre of
a large circle of their combined countrymen the spectators'
faces grave and silent since they apparently don't relish their
fights as the English do but see them rather as a duty to be
discharged with all the grim purpose of a mortuary assistant
cleaning a corpse

My larger crowd's assembling off to the side and there's
Lizzie Crosby arriving too with her hair bunched and her
ancient husband next to her in his full naval uniform like
he's about to watch a fucking regatta or something and her
kids six small copies of Crosby herself in numerous genders
and sizes with their faces scrubbed looking worried and a

pack of Mancs she's fooled into thinking she belongs with smiling and tall in the sun

The Russian lands his last slow blow and the Prussian slumps down flat before being dragged away by men who look like cousins or nephews the victor stares at the sky for a while then walks away to weep somewhere or I don't know write a poem so the mass of sad men move off and now it's our turn

Lizzie and I step into the middle

It's a group of a reasonable size that's turned out to watch the crowd from the pub the ones we picked up on the road German Fred's near the back I think I see Father Hearne in the middle and there's the furnace-stokers and Marcus lovely arms folded anxiously and lots more English too I turn about and look

All these faces encircling me

"Have you anything to say to me Annabel Donovan" says Lizzie her shoulders under her blouse are tense and bigger than I thought "Take back your accusation and we needn't fight today"

"Is that a hint of Lifford I hear in your accent there Lizzie" I say "I'll take nothing back my pig wants revenge now no tummy-shots and come at me"

Crosby shrieks and rushes she's a tall one but fast and this shocks me for a moment but then my muscles go aflame and I weave out the way I've not fought before like this but I've dodged enough drunken lurches outside The Angel on a Saturday night to deal with it deftly I step sideways and let Lizzie's own weight carry her groundward aiming a swift little kick into the small of her back as she goes down I could leap on her in the dirt and finish this now but I step back and give her the space to stand and brush the summer dust off let's not make this too easy the people need a show and she spits onto the flags and snorts hair coming un-bunched at the top and now she's back at me with scratches and my

hands go up to my face to push hers away but her sharp
middle fingernail catches the side of my neck and I feel the
tickle of a slow globe of blood sliding down it so I push her
back with my shoulder and punch her in the nose with my
left fist then in the chin with my right and then I open my
right hand because it hurts now and slam it into the side of
her head and she sways her hair even more undone then I'm
right up to her arms round her in an embrace and I hold on
tight laughing and we spin and spin clamped together before
I bite down as I hard as I can on one of those big shoulders
of hers she shrugs me away and I slap her face again and
cheekily wink and she rustles in her skirts and oh fuck is that
a hammer she's swinging and swinging at my belly and I
jump back and feel the air moving again and again as she
misses and then our eyes lock and I shout "No tummy-sh–"
but I don't get to finish the word because the claw of the
hammer hits my forehead and I fall back

Here are some of the things I think about as I topple down
I think about Marcus his lovely arms and his thighs
I think about my cellar and the pile of sawdust on the floor
where I sleep
I think about Pig Annie laughing
I think about food
I think about the grey fields where I'm from
I think about food
I think about my first long night in the cellar
I think about matches
I think about the music in The Dog and Duck
I think about how you can never be alone in this city
I think about my mother's thin hand in mine before she
closed her eyes
I think about the cart and the boat and the train
I think about Pig Annie snoring as we lay on the sawdust
together in the winter
I think about food
I think about the dirty dirty river
I think about Virgil's epic poem *The Aeneid* and how in

Virgil's epic poem *The Aeneid* Aeneas has to go his land is destroyed his people are defeated they're killed and captured and starved but he's protected by the Goddess of Love so he goes across the sea and he builds a new city and he makes that city the most important city in the world
I think about my father
I think about the little one and what happens next

There's blood in my eyes and there's Lizzie Crosby standing over me blocking out the sun crowing thinking we're done I let her get very close then grab her legs in mine and pull her down

And now I'm astride her thumping and thumping her head which bounces up off the flags each time her nose is spreading and my fists start hurting less she's staring at me and her children are screaming stop so I do and stand up

There's a lot of blood on her but I think it's mostly from me

I look down and her eyes are small and scared and her husband's saying "forgive her" but then I see the ring in her ear I see the ring and it's Pig Annie's silver ring that was my mother's ring I swear it is and so I bend and rip it out of her earlobe then stamp on her face again and again till her head goes soft and flops open on the flags

Silence.

Back in my cellar I lie on the sawdust

There's a knock at the door and Marcus comes through it and says "Annie what are you doing Lizzie's husband's gone to the Constabulary they'll be over here soon we have to leave now"

And I lie there in silence

"We have to leave now" he says and I'm silent

"I thought about going to my parents on the farm" he says "but it needs to be further Liverpool first then New York they'll be watching the station but one of the other stokers thinks he can borrow a horse"

I lie on the sawdust in silence

"Annie come on please I just want to see our child born in safety"

"There's no hope of safety Marcus" I say "The child could be born dead any second or born alive and die any second after that there could be a problem with the birth Marcus the child could be ill the child could be too hot in the day or too cold in the night maybe they go in their sleep suddenly or you roll over the child when you're drunk or I roll over the child when I'm drunk or one of us rolls over the child when we're not drunk or the child's hit by a cart or the child's bit by a dog or knocked by a shuttle or falls to the black-lung or gets worked to death or steps off a bridge because they're desolate or has nothing to eat has nothing to eat Marcus or the world just explodes one day for us and all of the children and what difference would it make if they're born in safety then"

"I don't have time to argue with you Annie I'll be back in a minute with the horse"

And he goes

And I lie on the sawdust and I can hear the green river Irk bubbling outside my cellar window in the early evening heat and my belly bubbles in reply

I stroke it then for the first time that very long day I stroke it gently with my sore hands and whisper "I really don't want the world to explode my darling my love

It's only two months till I meet you now it's only two months my darling

My love

And I can't wait"

Part Two

So Many Mornings

Place: Manchester City Centre.
Time: Saturday, 15 June 1996.

Cast

Various humans and non-humans in the city of Manchester on Saturday, 15 June 1996

This play is a kind of procession, or conveyor belt.

The tempo throughout is varied.

I

In room 414 of the dubiously graded three-star hotel The Britannia on Portland Street, Manchester, a middle-aged man from Türkheim, Bavaria, opens the thick smoke-heavy curtains and winces as loud sunlight strikes his eyes. He's apocalyptically hungover from the night before, when he consumed eight iced strawberry daquiris in the Blue Orchid Karaoke Lounge and belted out a surprisingly tuneful rendition of "Zombie" by The Cranberries with three South Korean students from the University of Manchester's biology faculty on backing vocals. His vision settles and he stares down into the road below. A street sweeper slowly clears last night's debris. Late shop assistants hurry to work. Buses push on past to Piccadilly Gardens. A girl walks home carrying her shoes. It's 9.07am on Saturday the fifteenth of June 1996. The weather is already very warm.

II

At a corner table in the restaurant downstairs an elderly couple from Newport, South Wales, tuck into their full English breakfasts. The clattering sound of cheap plates being stacked roughly echoes from the kitchen. The couple don't talk to each other, they rarely do at meals, these days. The husband slips his knife into his sausage and a hot jet of fat spurts out. They're both extremely happy.

III

Further down Portland Street in the just-opened Yates' sports bar a man in his sixties sips his first pint of the day. The England match doesn't start till 2pm so he'd probably better pace himself, but he isn't very good at taking his own advice and, besides, it's hot, you sober up quicker. He thinks about the national anthem, how he's not going to stand up for the national anthem. Whatever happens, there's no fucking way he's standing up for the national anthem, and that might cause a problem. But he'll be ten pints in by then, he won't care.

IV

At Piccadilly Gardens terminus a mum says, "Big jump!" and holds her four-year-old daughter's lollipop-sticky hand as she hops from the bus step down to the pavement. They thank the driver in unison and then start walking slowly towards Market Street still holding hands, and the daughter is excited, thinking about the shops.

V

At the top of Tib Street a 63-year-old woman in a fashionably oversized NOFX t-shirt says, "Today is the day that I finally do it. Today I will get my green hair."

VI

In a cramped room on the third floor of Affleck's Palace a magician, a real magician, not someone doing parlour tricks to impress people in pubs, but a long-haired man with command over the elements, a man with the power to reach into the very fabric of things and pull out a thread, stands before an assembled crowd of vaguely gothy-looking teenagers, eyeing them enigmatically. The bright light of the road has been shut out, there's a not-quite-strong-enough smell of incense to cover up the very strong smell of weed, and the magician opens his arms like a blessing and starts to speak in a deep and rasping voice. "Do you ever," he asks, "feel powerless? Does your life seem like somebody else's? Do you observe your own existence as if from under water, the small actions of which you are capable having no purchase at all on the indifferent cosmos? Well, I am here to say, my beautiful friends, that human beings are capable of anything. So let me tell you how to change the world . . ." It's 9.18am.

VII

In a burgundy Ford Granada heading up Regent Road over the Irwell three men sit listening to the radio. The passenger's leg twitches nervously next to the gearstick and the driver touches the twitching leg gently, to calm the passenger down.

VIII

In a corridor on the twenty-third floor of a tall building on Deansgate an estate agent grips a clipboard to her chest and knocks on a cream-coloured door for the seventh time in a row. She turns, frowning, to the couple behind her, two women in their late thirties, one of them holding a sleeping newborn baby. "The landlord promised they'd be in", she says. "I'm sorry."

IX

In a wood-panelled room facing the courtyard at Chetham's School of Music an eight-year-old cellist readies her instrument. Her sweaty hands slip on the tuning pegs. She didn't sleep at all last night. The cello feels heavier than usual and the examiner's eyes burrow into her uncomfortably, it's like he doesn't have any eyelids, she hasn't once seen this man blink, she feels a sudden urge to run away. There's a bird on a tree in the courtyard, she wants to go outside and look at the bird, play with the bird, maybe even be the bird, that would be nice, to loop and twirl about at the very top of the air, to leave whenever you like. Put the cello down and fly away. But then she thinks about her foster mum, thinks she'd probably get annoyed if she randomly turned into a bird to escape a man without any eyelids, so she looks at the notes on the page on the music-stand in front of her, breathes in, and starts to play.

X

In Saint Anne's Square an elderly gentleman riding a unicycle weaves through the shoppers. It's 9.23am.

XI

On the rink at the Nynex Arena the Manchester Storm ice hockey team's Russian goalkeeper stops a flying puck with his shin. He thinks about tonight, what he'll do after the match. He's heard there are lots of Russians in town for the Euros game against Germany tomorrow, so he'll go to a bar and hope he can run into some of them there. He's lonely in Manchester. His teammates are nice enough, but they don't seem to want to be friends, he invited them all round for soup one evening and only three of them came. His English isn't great, but it isn't appalling. Perhaps he'll never belong in Manchester. He's lived here for two years now but he'd still never say that he's from here. The people in Manchester seem to get very angry when someone says they're from Manchester who isn't from Manchester. He's heard you can only say you're from Manchester if you're from actual Manchester and not Greater Manchester, which means anyone from Stockport or Bury or Oldham or Bolton isn't from Manchester. If you're from Salford you're definitely not from Manchester. Didsbury is technically in Manchester, but you're not allowed to say you're from Manchester if you live there. If you live in Manchester but weren't born in Manchester, you're not allowed to say you're from Manchester. If you were born in Manchester but have ever left Manchester, including to go on holiday, then you're not allowed to say you're from Manchester, and if your parents aren't from Manchester then you're not from Manchester, which means that the only two people who are allowed to say they're from Manchester are the guy in the pub who outlined these criteria and the large inflatable Santa Claus that sits on top of the town hall at Christmastime. Are all new cities so exhausting? He flicks the puck back to the centre and waits for the next shot to come.

XII

In the Arndale Centre branch of the men's clothing store Stolen from Ivor a hairy man with an unruly goatee beard takes a half-price Hawaiian shirt down from the rack and looks at it, smiling. His wife shakes her head definitively and replaces the shirt on the rack.

XIII

In the doorway of Burger King on Piccadilly four teenagers survey the street in front of them, looking for someone to mug. The eldest among them is nearly fifteen, so they shouldn't attempt anyone older than that. Skaters are off the agenda, they can use their boards to whack you with, or whip you with their wallet-chains, one of them still has a big bruise from a fortnight ago, and they should avoid girls at all costs because girls are surprisingly strong for their size and are usually up for a fight. Best would be a posh lad on his own, strolling down the hill, off the train from Altrincham or somewhere, his voice would go all shaky when you speak to him, you'd say "look at me" and then when he did you'd say "don't fucking look at me" and you'd trick him like that, he'd usually cough up a tenner or so pretty quickly. Look, here comes one now, hair in curtains, navy blue shorts and moccasins on, The Great fucking Gatsby himself, come on lads, bunch my fist in my pocket, pretend it's a knife.

XIV

On King Street a young woman wearing a heart-shaped necklace walks past the fancy boutiques. She misses her dad, who is dead. It was bad two months ago, when her dad first died, but now it's worse, he's dead every day now. Her vision is fine, but a lot of the time she feels like she can't see. She doesn't remember having any breakfast. King Street is a blur. Apparently, these buildings here are shops. Apparently, she's walking along a road. Apparently, there is a person who exists, who is apparently her, who is walking along a road past some shops, apparently. What time is it? Does the time pass any quicker if she walks around some buildings that are apparently shops instead of going to bed for the rest of the day? Let's find out.

XV

On St Peter's Square in front of Central Library 37 ten-year-old boys all dressed as Liam Gallagher gather and sing. It's 9.34am.

XV

On St Peter's Square in front of Central Library 37 ten-year-old boys all dressed as Liam Gallagher gather and sing. It's 9.34am.

XVI

Inside the theatre on Cross Street the front of house manager stands on the stage and spins round. She likes to do this every single day before anyone else arrives, but she'd probably deny it if you asked her about it. She spins and looks at the seats and imagines people watching. She looks up through the hole above, through the big glass roof that goes out to the huge world beyond. So many mornings like this, she thinks. And mornings and mornings to come.

XVII

On the corner of Moseley Street and Charlotte Street a taxi driver rolls her eyes as a tall man is unable to get the mounted stag's head he's just purchased from an antique shop into her boot, due to the antlers. "Well, what am I supposed to do now?" asks the man.

XVIII

In a coffee shop on Princess Street an old woman asks for a cup of hot water, then sits at a table near the back of the shop. She takes a teabag out of a zip-lock packet, puts the teabag in the cup, and begins her day.

XIX

In Littlewoods on Market Street a shy woman stands in front of a mirror, smoothing down a new holiday dress.

XX

In Electronics Boutique in the Arndale the charismatic assistant manager flicks their hair and descants authoritatively to two impressed customers on the subject of pixelated breasts. "I find the jiggle-physics in Duke Nukem 3D overall to be satisfactory," they intone. "Of course there'd be sculpting issues around the nipples themselves, but the developers have cleverly avoided that through the use of tassels. If you're wanting a greater degree of verisimilitude to your boobs I would recommend getting yourself a decent graphics card, but a standard desktop word processor should be just fine under most circumstances, as long as you have 16 megs of RAM or more, I know, I know, the recommended specs say 8, but you won't get much mileage out of 8 megabytes of RAM these days, I personally have 64, and that does me just fine, although I do have to stress that upping your RAM won't make the boobs any clearer it'll just make the jiggles more smooth, and it's worth mentioning as well that 3D Realms, that's the developer, rather cynically, in my opinion, frontloads the boobs to the very first level of the game, which does make sense within the context, you know, we see the city descend from a kind of realism into a hellscape, and the diegetic music in the lap-dance club itself is a really fantastic touch, but you could probably get away with just playing the demo to be honest, and if you want my advice it's best to wait till next week anyway." "What's next week?" one of the customers asks timidly. "Wait there," says the assistant manager, heel-turning theatrically and heading into the back room of the shop, before emerging a few seconds later carrying a box of minimalist black design emblazoned with a large arcane symbol and the single word "Quake" across the top. The assistant manager grins. "This is going to change everything."

XXI

On Corporation Street a post-box glints red in the sunshine. It's 9.47am.

XXII

On Fountain Street a young man in a suit deftly fastens his tie as he heads hurriedly through the automatic doors to his office building. "I'm genuinely quite depressed," he thinks.

XXIII

In Parsonage Gardens a middle-aged woman watches the pigeons. She thinks about her son, who lives in Tasmania. Tasmania is very far away.

XXIV

In McDonald's in the Arndale Centre food court two teenage best friends slurp vanilla milkshakes and gaze at each other longingly for a second before snapping their eyes away. "When is he going to ask me out?" she thinks. "It's so obvious that I like him." "When is she going to ask me out?" he thinks. "It's so obvious that I like her."

XXV

On Albert Square outside the Town Hall an astonishingly beautiful man on rollerblades flashes past, almost too fast to see.

XXVI

In the Oxford Road branch of Kwik Save a very muscular bald man in a black vest is concerned about the other shoppers noticing he's buying yoghurt. He hasn't yet dared to approach the dairy section but has laid the groundwork by partially filling his basket with distractingly masculine items like cured sausage, Right Guard deodorant, Pot Noodles (beef flavour, of course) and apples, which are not particularly masculine in and of themselves but in their smooth rotundity somehow seem consonant with his own body shape and size. He makes his first tentative approach to the chilled food aisle but stops when he sees a small old woman laboriously selecting a block of cheese. She catches his eye and he tries to make an expression which connotes "Oh no, I appear to have forgotten something amid the vegetables" and he turns and retreats to the greengrocer section where he lurks unwillingly for half a minute or so pretending to size up a cabbage. He then returns to the chilled aisle only to find the old woman still there, squintingly scrutinising the ingredients label on a large block of cheddar, I mean what does she need to do that for, it's fucking cheddar for fuck's sake, so he goes and stands uncomfortably close to her, feigning interest in the virile Italian cheeses like Gorgonzola, until his looming bulk sends her scurrying, intimidated, towards the jams. He glances around to check the coast is clear before selecting and basketing the biggest yoghurt pot available, which, as if to add insult to injury, is pink, and covering it over with the bag of bulbous apples. He then realises, to his horror, that the sides of the basket are slatted, hence allowing lateral visibility into the basket, and that his various masculine distractive items, in their current arrangement, do not provide total coverage for the pink yoghurt pot. Given that he has approximately fifty metres to walk to the checkout in this extremely vulnerable condition, he moves to the more proximate magazine stand where he fashions a kind of makeshift gazebo out of a copy of last week's News of the World *and slips it over the top of the basket, blanketing the contents rather well. Pleased with his handiwork, he moves towards the tills, which are thankfully quite quiet, where his next task awaits him. The challenge here is to distract the checkout assistant, so at the precise moment she picks up and scans the yoghurt pot, she is too engaged by his sparkling conversation to notice that he's buying yoghurt and thus start laughing at him, and calling over everyone in the shop to come and laugh at him, and calling over everyone in the world to come and laugh at him and laugh at him, for being such a baby, for being such a fucking little girl, for buying yoghurt. "Hot today, isn't it?" he says, with his best charming smile. The cashier's eyes meet his just as the yoghurt barcode beeps. "Oh, we don't notice," she says. "There's air-con in here, you know." He bundles the offending pot into his rucksack, pays, and walks away briskly, ducking behind the passport photobooth as he does so, to avoid a guy he thinks he might know from the gym, and then he strolls back out through the sliding Kwik Save doors onto Oxford Road, where the morning sunlight pats his bald head warmly, as if to say well done.*

XXVII

In a private pool in a basement on Granby Row a happily divorced businesswoman swims up and down.

XXVIII

In a police helicopter high over the city a tactical flight officer surveys the streets below. Sunshine smiles off glass building-fronts, the blue oblongs of Magic Bus rooftops shuffle around like Tetris blocks, the proportion of men with their shirts off already seems high, even for a warm day in June. The officer watches a motorbike thread through the traffic on Deansgate. She wonders if she should get a motorbike, motorbikes are pretty cool, but helicopters are cool too, she supposes, remember when she went in to talk to her son's Year One class, all those wide-eyed six-year-olds, amazed that she can fly. That was a good day. She trains her binoculars onto a red and white Ford Cargo truck sitting stationary on Corporation Street and reaches for her radio. It's 9.59am, and she thinks she'll be here for a while.

XXIX

On a 192 bus pulling in near Piccadilly Station a fourteen-year-old girl sifts through coins in her purse. She wonders if the seven quid she has left over in pocket money is enough to buy her dad a decent card and present for Father's Day tomorrow. Or maybe she'll end up doing what she did last year and blowing the money in HMV then using a spare bit of printer paper and some of her brother's football stickers to "make" him a card. As long as she does him breakfast in bed he probably won't mind, and besides he did literally give her that money himself and say "this money's for you" so it'd be a bit ridiculous just to give it straight back to him in the form of a card he'll only throw away two days later and another pint-glass-shaped bottle opener he'll never use. No, she should get him a present. He's a good dad, he's an okay dad. Ugh. She walks down the hill towards Market Street. Ugh, Town's rammed though. Football later, Father's Day tomorrow, Queen's birthday today, why does everyone decide to go shopping just because some old lady they've never met's got a little bit older? It's particularly packed down here, though. Hang on, the road up ahead's blocked off. She goes up to a policewoman, standing outside Debenhams. "What's going on?" "Sorry, love, we're closing the city centre due to an ongoing incident." An ongoing incident? Great. "Any idea when you'll open it again?" The policewoman shakes her head. Fantastic. That's fantastic. Ugh. She stares at the other shoppers, milling about, and considers her options. Does she chance it with these lot or try and get the card and present somewhere else? She thinks for thirty seconds, then turns and heads back up the hill towards the 192 stop. There are card shops in Stockport, she can just go there. They have an HMV as well, as it happens.

XXX

In the shuttered doorway of a kebab shop on Shudehill a policewoman brusquely shakes a homeless man awake, to move him on. The homeless man groans and stands, before folding his thin sleeping bag under his arm and starting down towards Victoria Station. "Not that way," says the policewoman. "That way's closed."

XXXI

In River Island in the Arndale Centre the manager turns off the lights.

XXXII

*In the Disney Store in the Arndale Centre the manager turns off
the lights.*

XXXIII

In Our Price in the Arndale Centre the manager turns off the lights.

XXXIV

In Games Workshop in the Arndale Centre the manager turns off the lights. He gazes around at the empty shop. The place looks smaller in the dark. His own little empire. Boxes and boxes of intricate fantasy troops in plastic and metal, waiting to be taken home and constructed. The big display table in the middle of the store, laid out with its battle panorama. Green orcs in their silent phalanges. Impassive High Elves facing them. Each stern expression, each tusk or nose, each link on each chain on each chain-mail shirt individually hand-painted, by him. The dragon rider he only finished last night rearing up in the centre. The astroturf landscape, the pipe-cleaner trees, the river with its light foam of white spray-paint atop it, to indicate never-ceasing motion. "Oh, it's all so fragile!" he thinks. It's all so fragile. He leaves and locks the door. It's 10.27am.

XXXV

On the corner of St Mary's Gate and Corporation Street a big Alsatian police dog breathes and waits. Sounds and smells converge, and she tries to isolate them. The bright, evacuated road in front of her stretches out clean and far. The lead is unclipped from her collar, and she runs.

XXXVI

Outside a Turkish café on John Dalton Street the manager hands out tall glasses of water to people standing around. She'd be working anyway right now, but these people, they can't get home. They can't get anywhere. The traffic's at a standstill, the centre's been cleared and blocked off. She'd be working anyway, though. And she's grateful for something to do. Once they've run out of glasses, she'll stay outside and talk to these people. Sometimes you just do what you'd normally do, and it helps. She sends one of the waitresses into the kitchen, to fetch some food.

XXXVII

In the long queue to use the phone box on St Peter's Square a short man with his shirt off makes jokes. He begins with some sarcasm referring to the unusual weather, before moving on to some more topical stuff about the England–Scotland game this afternoon, questioning the potential match-fitness of various players due to their well-known issues with alcohol, before feeling bold enough to riff light heartedly on the subject of the queue members themselves and their respective appearances, envisaging, with increasingly exaggerated absurdity, their reasons for needing the phone. His audience is quiet at first, consumed with their own anxieties, failing to register his voice as directed towards them, but eventually tuning in to the specific flights of his wild imagination with titters, then chuckles, then guffaws. A woman wearing a pink baseball cap says he should be a stand-up, and he lowers his eyes demurely, flattered, but thinks that will never happen. No: small spontaneous gestures of hilarity in times of public stress, that is his forte. A departures lounge during a long flight delay, a railway station platform when a train gets cancelled. Here, now. Others may think differently, but for him there is no better thing in the world than standing with some people he'll never see again, making them laugh.

XXXVIII

*At the bottom of Deansgate three tracksuited teenagers offer their
place on a wall to a wheezing woman, so she can sit down. It's
10.46am.*

XXXIX

On Piccadilly Gardens the great bronze statue of Queen Victoria wrinkles her nose disgustedly as a group of confused German football fans sweat on her plinth. It's 10.52am.

XL

On King Street a little boy can't find his mother. It's 11.01am.

XLI

On Corporation Street a remote-controlled British Army robot moves on slow caterpillar treads towards its target. It's 11.06am.

XLII

In the small public cemetery at Manchester Cathedral the silent dead sleep on. There aren't any headstones to remember them by, they were all bombed to bits in the War, but the bones in the ground remember, and the soil changed by the bones in ground, and the city changed by the soil. 1583. 1649. 1721. 1819. 1846. The city remembers them all. It's 11.11am.

XLIII

At the top of Market Street a twenty-one-year-old photography student raises her SLR camera and takes a photo, then another, before everything vanishes into the past.

XLIV

*On the corner of Cross Street and St Anne Street a heavily
pregnant woman is starting to get annoyed. Her feet hurt and no
one really knows what's going on. The police look bored and claim
they don't know anything. Everyone's just standing around, which
you can't really blame them for, but it's still very annoying. She's
very tired. Unusual combinations of people are chatting to each
other, there's some goths chatting to an old man wearing war
medals over there, someone drunk's laughing with the police, but
she's too annoyed to get involved in any of that. The baby's kicking
again. Not now please, baby. She gazes up Cross Street in front of
her, there's something moving up there, and she takes a few steps
forward to get a better view, and someone behind her shouts. It's
11.17am on Saturday the fifteenth of June 1996, and an almighty
boom breaks the air and sucks everything inwards.*

*The goths and the veteran, the drunk and the police, the buildings
and the streets and the streetlights and the windows and the offices
and the bus stops and the cafés and the homes and the shops and
everything in the shops, the people and everything they want,
everyone they're here with, the people people love, the city on this hot
June day, the woman who stepped forward to see what's going on.*

Oh, it's all so fragile!

And she goes up, up, up into the air . . .

Part Three

Coming Home

*Place: Saint Michael's Flags and Angel Meadow Park,
Manchester.*

Time: Now.

Cast

Kaz – a woman from the West of Ireland

Jenny – a woman from Manchester

Little Girl in an Angel Costume – Kaz's daughter, 8 years old

The tempo throughout is slower.

*Present day. Saint Michael's Flags and Angel Meadow Park,
Manchester. Two women,* **Jenny** *and* **Kaz***, are seated at opposite
ends of a bench. There's a thick A4-sized purple folder next to*
Jenny *on the bench, but she's staring off into space.* **Kaz** *is
watching her eight-year-old daughter play nearby. The little girl is
wearing an angel costume, and she's running around in circles, lost
in her own little world. She starts to stray off a bit.*

Kaz Annie

Annie don't go too far now

Silence.

Good girl

It's late we should head back soon

Silence.

Jenny Excuse me

Kaz Yes

Jenny Are you Irish

Silence.

Kaz Yes

Silence.

Jenny I'm Irish too

Kaz Oh

Lovely

Silence.

Jenny Excuse me again

Kaz Yes

Jenny You know how I said I was Irish before

That was a lie

I don't know why I said that

I'm not Irish

Kaz   Okay

Silence.

Jenny   Well my dad's Irish and I have an Irish last name

Kaz   So you are Irish

Jenny   Well I have a passport so I guess technically I am but I only got that because I was angry about Brexit and I don't sound Irish obviously and I've only been to Ireland once and that was for a riverboat cruise on the Shannon when I was eleven so I really don't think that qualifies me to be actually Irish and I'm very sorry I lied to you just now

Silence.

Do you forgive me

Kaz   It's not a big deal

Silence.

Jenny   I do it all the time

Weird exaggerations unnecessary little lies

I wait fifteen minutes for a bus in the rain then tell the driver it's been twenty

Just find myself saying a more impressive number you know

Kaz   Maybe you are Irish then

Jenny   I work in insurance so I suppose I'm used to people rounding things up

Can you forgive me though

I'd really like it if you could

Silence.

Kaz   Of course I can

I do

Silence.

Jenny   I don't feel very Irish

Kaz   I'm not sure Irish is an emotion

Jenny   My name is Jenny by the way

Kaz   I'm Kaz

Silence.

Jenny

I love this park at the start of the evening

I come here all the time

Jenny   Is this your daughter

Kaz   Yes

Jenny   I like her outfit

Kaz   There's a Swiss-German painter Paul Klee

She's completely obsessed

Eight-year-olds are very very brilliant

Jenny   I've actually got a flat viewing nearby

Kaz   Oh which building

Jenny (*points*)   That one

It's a warehouse conversion

Kaz   Fancy

Jenny   My boyfriend's meeting me there with the estate agent

But I had some stuff to do in Town beforehand

I arrived very early so I thought I'd sit here for a bit

I grew up in Manchester but I've never been to this park before

Kaz   Saint Michael's Flags and Angel Meadow

It's historic

Jenny   So all the materials say

She starts looking through her folder.

Endlessly droning on about the so-called "industrial heritage"

Kaz   Ugh that's gross

Jenny   Here take a look at this

She hands her a pamphlet from the folder.

Kaz (*reading*)   "Angel One apartments

Situated fashionably in a former tobacco factory these spacious two- and three-bedroom units offer the best of contemporary city centre living in an environment filled with desirable period features that oozes historical charm

A stylish open-plan industrial-living setting that reminds you why Manchester was once the most important city in the world

So come and join the new Industrial Revolution

Concierge basement gym etcetera" I think I was just a little bit sick in my mouth

Jenny I'm sorry

But it baffles me that anyone would actually want to live somewhere like that

Jenny   Why

Exposed brickwork is very popular these days

Kaz   "In the dark of the night you can hear the ghostly screams of overworked Victorian orphans oozing historical charm"

Jenny   I'm actually quite partial to a visible joist myself

Kaz   The scene of decades of processed death but never mind that everybody there's a concierge

Jenny   I was very excited about the concierge to be honest Kaz

Kaz   I don't think this friendship is going anywhere I'm sorry

They smile. Silence.

Kaz   No I do understand the appeal

Did you see the boards over there

I love this park but it used to be Hell in the past

Bare-knuckle fights here every weekend

Then it was a giant paupers' grave

There's forty thousand people buried here you know

Most of them probably Irish

Jenny   Wow

Kaz   I mean

Forty thousand

My daughter had a picture book when she was small

Six acrobats

Twenty balloons

I don't even think I can imagine what forty thousand actually looks like

Say all their names out loud you'd be here for twenty-two hours

Silence.

But still

I love this park

Silence.

It's peaceful here

Jenny   Do you think the city's forgotten

Kaz   I don't think a place can forget

Jenny   Or healed

Kaz   Healed

I don't know

Silence.

You're moving back to Manchester then

Jenny   I am

Well I didn't grow up in the centre but I came here a lot as a kid

Kaz   Where were you before

Jenny   London

Kaz   What was that like

Jenny   Monstrous

Sprawling

You never really know where you are in London

You get the Tube and pop up in all these different places but none of it hangs together

Manchester's nice because the centre's so small

I can visualise every single street

It's all on a map in my head you know

My boyfriend Danny's not from here so I told him I'd take charge of the flat-hunting

Kaz   Hence the very serious folder

Jenny   Hence the very serious folder yes

Look

Colour-coded tabs

Dozens of city-centred properties ranked and assessed in various criteria

People think finding a flat in a fastmoving market's all about luck but it's not

The chance of an optimal outcome is greatly increased by adequate preparation

Kaz   Spoken like a true insurance agent

Jenny   I get a bit overexcited about this stuff

I couldn't believe we'd be living here in Town

I used to get the bus here every Saturday and now I'd be rolling out of bed and into the Arndale

It felt like a dream

Silence.

I was going to have a baby

We thought we'd move back to be nearer my parents

Got rid of our flat down in London

Shifted our jobs up here

But then

Silence.

Kaz   I'm sorry

Silence.

Jenny   No I'm sorry

Talking about this to a stranger

Silence.

Kaz   I think it's good to talk about these things

Long silence.

Would you like a dried apricot

She takes out a packet of dried apricots and opens it and puts it down on the bench between them. They take a couple and eat them. The little girl comes over and takes one too. **Jenny** *watches the little girl.* **Kaz** *watches* **Jenny** *watching the little girl.*

I moved here a decade ago

I'm an artist and there wasn't lots there for me on the west coast of Ireland

When I was little my grandmother used to tell me stories about her two sisters

My great-aunts

The two of them moved to Manchester together in August 1940

Pitched up at the Midland Hotel and were hired on the spot as chambermaids

Their first night on the job was the first night of the Blitz

They spent it hiding under the stairs with some of the guests as the bombs rained down

Drinking champagne out of room-service teacups

I used to love that story about the champagne in the teacups and so I think Manchester always held a kind of earthy glamour for me as a result

I moved here on my own and got a job behind a bar in the Northern Quarter

I'd paint in the day and at night I'd hand bottles of beer to tall people in berets

And I'd sleep at some point or other

If you'd asked me at the time I'd have said I was lonely and miserable but looking back it was exhilarating and I'm amazed at how energetic and determined I was

Once I was dancing at Warehouse Project and there was a very sweaty boy dancing next to me in this extraordinarily angular manner it was like he was some kind of gigantic human elbow

We went back to mine and it was lovely and in the morning the elbow left and I never asked for his number because he lived in a different city and sometimes moments are just perfect as they are

I was very surprised to be pregnant and for a long time I was in denial about it I mean we were careful and I didn't tell my mum for nearly six months and she was angry she's still never forgiven me for that and for not going home and I do understand her it must be so so hard to be so far away with nothing you can do

And then suddenly it appeared I had a daughter

Silence.

Jenny   She's never met her father

Kaz   I don't know how I'd get in touch with him

But to be perfectly honest with you I've never even tried

Sometimes I feel bad about it you know

It's like I'm keeping half her history from her

But ultimately I love that our life is just the two of us and I don't want to change it

I suppose that makes me a terrible person

Silence.

We live in the big concrete tower at the top end of Deansgate

Jenny   I know the one

Kaz   It still manages to be cheap because there's a brothel somewhere in the building but the location of the brothel keeps changing so the police can never shut it down

Every day I'm grateful for that brothel

Jenny   After the bomb in Ninety-Six

That's when they started regenerating everything

Putting up all these newbuilds

Converting all the old mills and factories

Your place would've been around before then

That's another reason why it's still cheap

Not new enough for "contemporary living"

Not old enough for "historical charm"

Kaz   Were you here for the bomb in Ninety-Six

Jenny   I was

Well I wasn't in town

Kaz   Do you remember it

Jenny   No

I mean I was nine

It was hot and everyone was in the garden but I don't remember a sound or anything

I remember I was grumpy when they cancelled *Bugs* on the telly that night

I wasn't here for the other bomb

Were you

Kaz   Yes

I was at home that night

I do remember the sound

Silence.

God

Silence.

I was pregnant with her at the time

I was incredibly scared

Silence.

The city's changed so much even since then

Have you been down Oxford Road recently

Jenny   Are you going to tell me it looks like New York

Because everyone always says that

Kaz   No

I was going to say Dubai

But I guess you get the picture

Jenny   I was in town yesterday as well in fact

For my induction at my firm's Manchester office

Older bloke from Levenshulme showed me round

It's a shiny building on Fountain Street this office and I asked him if we'd always been based here and he said no we used to be over on Corporation Street but that office got destroyed thirty years ago by the bomb

And it was a shock just hearing that word

Even the sound of it puts violence into a sentence and it was the first time anyone had mentioned it to me in ages

And then I asked the bloke if he worked for the company at the time and he said that he did

And then I asked the bloke if he was in the office on that day and he said that he was

And I thought for a second that maybe I should change the subject but then I found myself asking him anyway just you know because I couldn't help it I asked him

What was it like

And then he went quiet for a very long time

And then he said that it was loud

Silence.

He said he shouldn't have been in the office on a Saturday morning but he had a few bits to finish off from the week and quite lot of other people did too

And the police did a marvellous job evacuating the Arndale and the station and the M&S and the theatre and the whole city centre but there was this one office block right next to the truck with the bomb in it but nobody told them to leave because it was a Saturday and when they looked in the windows the receptionist wasn't there so they just thought it must be empty

But it wasn't

So there he was reading through claims thinking about the nice cold pint he'd have afterwards in the pub watching England when all of a sudden

The world explodes

Silence.

And I asked him if he was hurt and he said thankfully not too badly just a few little cuts but this is an old Mancunian bloke we're talking about so there was definitely an element of trying to appear hard there

He said others had it far far worse than he did

But nobody died

And then I asked him if he still thinks about it and he said every day

He said he thinks about it every single day

His back gate goes in the wind and he's there at his desk in the wreckage again

He has to excuse himself from his grandson's fifth birthday because he's anxious about the balloons and people say that it was the best thing that ever happened to Manchester it looks so shiny and new now and nobody died and nobody died and nobody died

But it never went away

Not for that man in my office

When something that huge happens in your life I don't know how anyone ever

Silence.

How anyone ever

Silence.

And so I went home and I stayed up all night working on my very serious purple flat-hunting folder

Silence.

Kaz   Was it weird being Irish

Back in Ninety-Six

Jenny   I'm not Irish

I have an Irish last name like half of this city

Kaz   Weird for your dad then

Jenny   It was a weird time

For ages afterwards you couldn't go a weekend without
someone saying their mum's dentist used to play
backgammon with Gerry Adams' former hygienist and she
says don't go to the Trafford Centre on Saturday

And so we'd stay at home

My dad was in the Army and we had a big stick next to the
front door with a mirror on it and he told me it was for golf
but it was actually for checking for car bombs

Kaz   That's intense

Jenny   He didn't open the curtains during the day for most
of the Eighties and Nineties

Kaz   Irish in the British Army

Okay

How does your dad feel about that

Jenny   I don't know

He always gets annoyed if I ask him about it

Kaz   And how do you feel about it

Jenny   I don't know it's really complicated

I guess I see why he joined

He wanted to belong

Silence.

How's it been for you

Being here

Being Irish

Kaz   I didn't come here till 2016 things were already so
different by then

Some of the old stereotypes still persist I suppose

People think you like drinking and fighting

A presumed fascination with root vegetables

Things are generally more subtle than that these days though

A certain suspicion at the sound of your name

Maybe you get that too

Somebody's Christmas present goes missing at your new boyfriend's house and you're the first one to be questioned

But it's better than it was

So many things are

Silence.

Have you ever read Friedrich Engels

Jenny   I haven't

Kaz   Nineteenth-century German sociologist used to live round here

Claimed the Irish were obsessed with pigs for some reason

I've no idea what that was all about

I suppose the way I see it is if you tell people there's a better life waiting for them when they get here

Then cram them into attics into cellars

And work them into the ground

And give them nothing to hope for and nothing to eat and nowhere to be

Then what do you expect

They'll want to drink

They'll want to fight

They'll want to fight you

They'll hurt you over and over again until you listen to them

What do you expect

Silence.

And now everyone wants the passport so they can move to Portugal or whatever

Silence.

It's better than it was

Silence.

Jenny   Danny's determined to start trying again immediately

I don't want to

Kaz   How's he doing

Jenny   He's mostly okay

He cries a lot

Anyone who says men don't cry enough should watch one lose a baby

He's doing a lot of cross-fit

He's really fed up with people telling him to go to therapy all the time

Kaz   And how are you

Silence.

You're not here early for the viewing

You missed it didn't you

Jenny   I'm twenty minutes late

I got here on time but I couldn't set foot in the lobby

I kept on thinking about the man in my office

I kept thinking that nobody died

I kept thinking I was careful so careful that there is a most careful person in the world and it's me I never ate oysters or any shellfish at all or cured meat or cheese with the rind on it I turned down the half-glass of prosecco at my leaving do I planned and I mitigated and I calculated and I assessed because that's who I am but none of that matters in the slightest when they finally go to listen and there isn't any heartbeat at all

Silence.

Everyone says that when you do eventually have your baby it'll be even better

That the new one will only be who they are because of the one you lost

And that's some kind of tremendous gift

And then you will be so glad

But I don't want to be glad

I don't want the good thing to come and erase the bad

I don't want to be glad

I don't want to be glad

So no I'm not going to the viewing

I'm not doing anything at all

I'm not moving

This stillness and silence is my house now forever

Kaz   But you're not being still

You got up in the morning

You put on your clothes and your shoes

And you're here

In a place that's been bombed and bombed and bombed but is somehow more beautiful than ever

And you're talking to me

Jenny   In the explosion on Corporation Street a pregnant woman was thrown four point six metres into the air and her baby was born safe and well two weeks later and she was called Kay-Leigh

Kaz   That's a lovely name

Silence. **Jenny** *stands.*

Jenny   I hate you Kaz

I really fucking absolutely loathe you

Kaz *stands and hugs* **Jenny***. They hug for a very long time. They start to turn while they're hugging, till eventually they're spinning round and round. They spin and spin, then they stop and let go.* **Kaz** *touches* **Jenny***'s shoulder.*

Kaz   I think you should go to the viewing

Jenny   I don't know if I can

Kaz   I'm not a particularly religious person

But when I heard that huge sound that night from my window

I found myself suddenly frantically

Praying

For me

For her

For everyone out there

People think hope's something quiet and heroic

A warm little light in the evening

Not in my book

Not when you're feeling it it isn't

Hope in the moment of hoping just feels like

Fear

Silence.

Jenny   Why are you so

Silence.

Kaz   If you go now you might still catch them

Jenny *makes to go but then stops.*

Jenny   Kaz can I ask you a question

What's it like

Being a mum

Silence.

Kaz (*with deep, deep compassion*)   It's wonderful

Jenny *takes a sad moment, and then she moves off hurriedly.* **Kaz** *watches her go. Silence.* **Kaz**'*s daughter moves towards the bench.*

Little Girl in Angel Costume   She left her folder mum

What should we do

Kaz   Let's leave it in case she comes back

Little Girl in Angel Costume   Do you think she's going to get there

Silence.

Kaz   I don't know

Silence. **Kaz** *turns round and takes a long look at the audience.*

It's (*she looks at her watch, then says the time and date right now, as this is happening, as the audience are watching the show, in the following format – "It's [time] am/pm on the [number] of [month], [year]."*)

And then she looks at her daughter.

Come on my darling

Come on my love

Let's go home

They leave together, slowly.

Emptiness for a while.

The sounds of the park, then the sounds of the city, getting louder.

Acknowledgements

Thank you –

To the brilliant Selina Cartmell, for setting it all in motion.

To Emily McLaughlin, for asking excellent questions.

To Alistair McDowall and Sam Pritchard, for their early enthusiasm.

To Dean Kirby, whose bracing book *Angel Meadow: Victorian Britain's Most Savage Slum* was a key resource for the historical detail in the first part of the play.

To everyone who shared with me their memories and experiences of 15th June 1996.

To my amazing agent, Rachel Taylor, as ever, as always.

To my hero James Macdonald, for whom nothing is impossible.

To Elaine Cassidy & Kat Pearce & Fionnuala Dorrity & Laura Hopkins & Charles Balfour & Ian Dickinson & Georgina Lamb & Katie Greenall & Sadie Mears & Jacqui Leigh & Sarah Smith & Alex Burke & Amelia Blackburn & T Harris & Scott Macdonald & tireless Amy Chandler & Michael Betteridge & everyone at the Royal Exchange & all the community company and volunteers, literally hundreds of people, whose generosity and commitment is a testament to their love for this extraordinary city and its extraordinary theatre.

Finally, to my whole family, particularly to Lucy Jackson, for Everything, and to my great-aunts Margaret and Bridie, who came across the sea, to Manchester.

Rory Mullarkey, April 2026